ARVEL®

ULTIMATE X-MEN

VOL 15

MAGICAL

-RANEY-

ISANOVE

**ULTIMATE X-MEN VOL. 15: MAGICAL.** Contains material originally published in magazine form as ULTIMATE X-MEN #72-74 and ANNUAL #2. First printing 2007. ISBN# 0-7851-2020-3. Published by MARVEL PUBLISHING, INC., a subsidiary of MARVEL ENTERTAINMENT, INC. OFFICE OF PUBLICATION: 417 5th Avenue, New York, NY 10016. Copyright © 2006 and 2007 Marvel Characters, Inc. All rights reserved. $11.99 per copy in the U.S. and $19.25 in Canada (GST #R127032852); Canadian Agreement #40668537. All characters featured in this issue and the distinctive names and likenesses thereof, and all related indicia are trademarks of Marvel Characters, Inc. No similarity between any of the names, characters, persons, and/or institutions in this magazine with those of any living or dead person or institution is intended, and any such similarity which may exist is purely coincidental. **Printed in Canada.** ALAN FINE, President & CEO Of Marvel Toys and Marvel Publishing, Inc.; DAVID BOGART, VP Of Publishing Operations; DAN CARR, Executive Director of Publishing Technology; JUSTIN F. GABRIE, Managing Editor; STAN LEE, Chairman Emeritus. For information regarding advertising in Marvel Comics or on Marvel.com, please contact Joe Maimone, Advertising Director, at jmaimone@marvel.com or 212-576-8534.

10 9 8 7 6 5 4 3 2 1

# ULTIMATE
# X-MEN

## MAGICAL

Writer
**Robert Kirkman**
Issues #72-74
Penciler (breakdowns on #73-74):
**Tom Raney**
Inker (finishes on #73-74):
**Scott Hanna**
Colors:
**Gina Going-Raney with June Chung**
Letters:
**Virtual Calligraphy's Joe Caramagna**
Covers:
**Tom Raney & Richard Isanove**

Annual #2 Art:
**Salvador Larroca**
Art, Bonus Feature:
**Leinil Francis Yu**
Colors:
**Jason Keith**
Colors, Bonus Feature:
**Dean White**
Cover:
**Salvador Larroca & Richard Isanove**

Associate Editor:
**John Barber**
Editor:
**Ralph Macchio**

Collection Editor:
**Jennifer Grünwald**
Assistant Editor:
**Michael Short**
Associate Editor:
**Mark D. Beazley**
Senior Editor, Special Projects:
**Jeff Youngquist**
Vice President of Sales:
**David Gabriel**
Production:
**Jerron Quality Color**
Vice President of Creative:
**Tom Marvelli**

Editor in Chief:
**Joe Quesada**
Publisher:
**Dan Buckley**

Born with strange and amazing abilities, the X-Men are young mutant heroes, sworn to protect a world that fears and hates them.

On being tested by the Church of Shi'ar Enlightenment, Jean Grey has learned that she is mentally unbalanced—not the immensely powerful entity known as the Phoenix, which the Shi'ar worship as a god. Jean is being kept under observation in the X-Mansion's infirmary until it can be determined that she is not a threat to her fellow students.

Meanwhile, Elliot Boggs—the new X-Man known as Magician—has taken the world by storm. This popularity followed an auspicious debut—the teenager was dropped onto the X-Men's doorstep by Nick Fury (head of the superhuman defense initiative called the Ultimates) after the first manifestation of Elliot's powers (inadvertently) killed his parents. In the time since his arrival, Elliot has become a media darling, bringing the X-Men back into the spotlight.

But Elliot and the X-Men aren't the only people in Professor Charles Xavier's world. Some months ago, he had a rather unusual meeting with a rather unique mutant...

# MAGICAL
## PART 1 (OF 3)

Westchester General Hospital.

Ugn.

Oh, God... That twit *stabbed* me, *didn't* she?

Oh, hey, *Elf.* Where're the rest of Charlie's Angels? The hallway? At home having a party?

You the only one? Is Warren here?

Kurt?

Kurt?

**Panel 1:** Maybe you could show *me* a few of those moves sometime. Lord knows I could *use* some improvement in my fighting. What do you say?

**Panel 2:** You've twisted my arm.

Anytime, Kitty. Just say the word.

**Panel 3:** Don't you *have* a boyfriend already?

Shut up.

**Panel 4:** Are you *okay*? You seem preoccupied.

**Panel 5:** It's nothing, really.

Thinking about *Jean.*

BEEP BEEP

**Panel 6:** Yes? It's done. We're on our way back to the Mansion now. Yes, sir. At present speed? No more than ten minutes. Yes, sir.

**Panel 7:** What was *that* about?

The Professor, seeing when we'll be back at the Mansion. That's odd, he *never* checks up on us like that.

**Panel 8:** Maybe something is wrong.

ISSUE 74

# MAGICAL
## CONCLUSION

Possible? I think we've discovered today that what is *possible* is far beyond anything we could *ever* have imagined.

There is a lot to learn from this incident. Let's hope the lessons from today help us live through the inevitable events of tomorrow.

We need to be more vigilant in our recruitment efforts. Not just in who we accept into this school but to monitor mutants across the world-- immediately, as their powers manifest.

Mutant powers are a *gift*, I truly believe that. But Magician has proven to us that our understanding of the *limits* of mutant ability is rudimentary at best.

Simply put--there *are* none.

Left unchecked, Elliot Boggs could have unwillingly caused the deaths of us all--or hundreds, if not thousands, of people.

We have to be prepared to do what must be done in the event of such mutants manifesting.

I'll send a team over to scan the area--there must be a trace of him here...something to indicate he *existed*.

Something for his parents to *bury*.

New York City.

**Your** power isn't **so** impressive. I'm sure I could figure it out. Reading people's minds? That's not so hard.

Oh? Then give it a shot, if you think so.

Let's peer through that impressive dome or yours to see what's inside-- ah, I see. You're thinking about my kooky religion. You don't understand how someone as obviously intelligent as me could fall for such an outlandish fairy tale.

"Giant cosmic bird"--I bet that's run through your head once or twice.

Hm. Not quite.

But close?

Quite the contrary, actually. In fact, I think the origins of the Shi'ar religion is one of the most fascinating things I've **ever** heard.

You don't think it's far-fetched?

ISSUE 2

# PREVIOUSLY IN ULTIMATE X-MEN

Born with strange and amazing abilities, the X-Men are young mutant heroes, sworn to protect a world that fears and hates them.

One member of the team—Alison Blaire, better known as the punk singer, Dazzler—has been in a coma for the past sev[en] weeks, after she was injured in battle.

Her teammate, Nightcrawler, has been acting unusually since Dazzler's injury, frequently holding vigil in her hospital [room].

Before joining the X-Men, Nightcrawler had been forced into working as an agent for the black-ops unit called Weapo[n X] which tortured mutants and turned them into killers...

# BREAKING POINT

BRAKKA! BRAKKA! BRAKKA! BRAKKA!

BRAKKA! BRAKKA! BRAKKA!

BAMF

SVAAASH!!

No, sir. It should be done by now. I don't know what the delay is. We'll circle around one more time--any longer and they'll have their fighters in the air. I don't--

BAMF

Never mind, sir.

Mission accomplished.

Hellooo?! Earth to Kurt?!

You in there?!

Oh my God, Ali! I'm so glad you're avake!

You are in great *danger*-- it's not safe here!

You must come vith *me*! Ve must hurry! They vill find us here--kill us!

You've got to go into hiding vith me!

Gah-- what?!

What are you--?!

BAMF

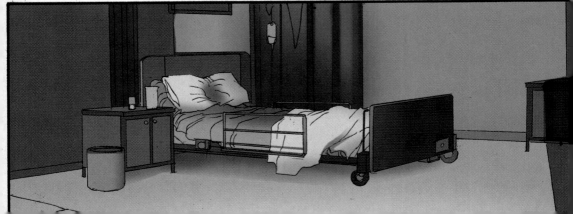

Are you okay?

Chuck, please. Are you *really* asking me that? I've taken care of business like that before. More than I can even remember... and let me tell you, as many as I *remember*--I must have done it a *lot*.

This ain't somethin' I'm *proud* of, don't get me wrong...but I don't regret it one bit. I saved the lot of you, remember?

So *yeah*... I'm just *fine*.

I haven't even given it a second thought.

Logan, I'd be a *fool* to ignore what kind of man you were when you came here. You were originally sent to *kill* me, after all. But I like to think your time here has *changed* you.

At least somewhat.

Do I expect you to be upset? *No.* But I would very much like to hear that you've at least given the fact a second thought.

If it helps your sense [of] accomplishment--sure. I'd do it [agai]n in a heartbeat, but part of me [wishe]s the kid could have just listened [to yo]u and not tried to kill everyone.

Thank you.

We done here?

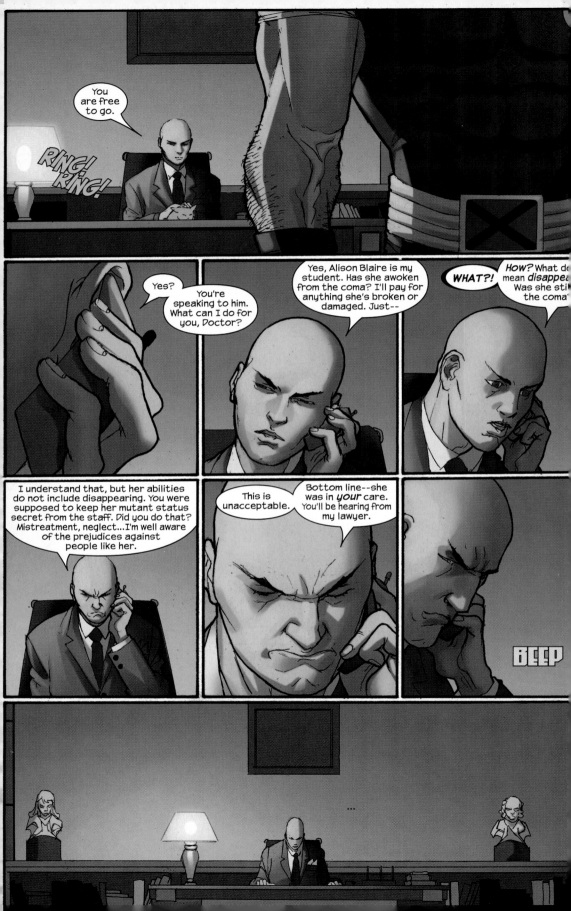

Alison Blaire is *missing.*

She disappeared from her room yesterday afternoon. The hospital had been trying to get in touch with me--and for obvious reasons, couldn't until a few minutes ago.

We don't know what happened to her. We don't know if she's awake or still in her coma. We don't know *where* she could have gone.

If she has awoken from her coma, it wouldn't be unlike her to just disappear without letting us know.

We may have nothing to worry about.

So what's with the meeting, then?

If you'd let me *finish,* Bobby.

⁵Ahem!⁵

We *may* not have anything to worry about, but I want to be *sure.* I'm going to the hospital to scan the minds of the staff there--to make sure there's no foul play involved.

I'd like the rest of you to take a quick trip out to the local clubs Dazzler played in. See if anyone's *heard* from her.

**Dismissed.**

**Chuck.**

**Yes.**

I hate to even bring it up--but our boy Kurt, when I was close to him...

He *reeked* of our missing tattooed friend. It was a *fresh* scent, too.

...under *no* circumstances are you to use deadly force.

*None.*

I mean it.

You, more than anyone, know what Weapon X do to someone psyche.

I get it. Kurt is one of us. Don't worry.

I *know*, I sensed it on him the moment he entered the room. I'm assembling a team telepathically as we speak.

You can meet them in the hangar in two minutes. You are more than welcome to join them, but Wolverine...

S'okay, kid. You get *one* free one......but just *one*.

Stop this, friend. Come back with us--let us *help* you, *please*.

We are not your enemies. We're your *friends*.

I vant to hear that from *you* least of all. I don't even vant to hear the sound of your *voice*. Vhat you *are*--vwhat you *hid* from me...

...it *sickens* me.

That is *enough!*

Peter-- *NO!*

Stand back, Scott. I will put this man in his place. I have held back *enough.*

Enough!!

BAMF

AMF

I hate that you've brought me to *this!*

BAMF

NO!! Not until I--! --irk!

OH, GOD!!

Ngg.

GGH!!

Oh, help me--

--get--

--him out of my--

BAMF

BAMF

--head!

YEAARGH!!

ROGUE!!

Oh, God, Bobby...oh, God.

My powers are back...

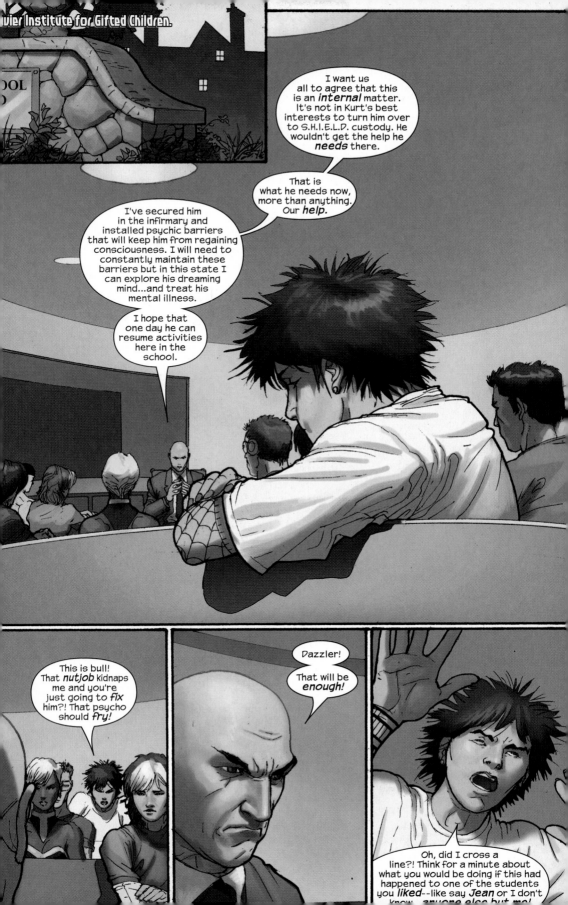

The Professor doesn't want us in here...and I don't even know if you can hear me anyway...so I'll make this *quick.*

I know what it's like to grow up being a mutant. To have people treat you a certain way just because you're different. I know about the ridicule, the isolation.

I know that it must be especially hard when you *look* different too. People who judged you just by the way you look...they probably thought you were a *monster.*

I just wanted to say that after being in your head... seeing what you *really* are...on the inside...

I *know* you're a monster.

**SKETCH A**

**SKETCH B**

**PENCILS**

**SKETCH C**

# THE ULTIMATE MARVEL LIBRARY

## ULTIMATE DAREDEVIL AND ELEKTRA

**ULTIMATE DAREDEVIL AND ELEKTRA VOL. 1 TPB...$11.99**
(ISBN: 0-7851-1076-3)

**ULTIMATE ELEKTRA: DEVIL'S DUE TPB...$11.99**
(ISBN: 0-7851-1504-8)

## THE ULTIMATES

**VOL. 1: SUPER-HUMAN TPB...$12.99**
(ISBN: 0-7851-0960-9)

**VOL. 2: HOMELAND SECURITY TPB...$17.99**
(ISBN: 0-7851-1078-X)

## THE ULTIMATES 2

**VOL. 1: GODS AND MONSTERS TPB...$14.99**
(ISBN: 0-7851-1093-1)

## ULTIMATE FANTASTIC FOUR

**VOL. 1: THE FANTASTIC TPB...$12.99**
(ISBN: 0-7851-1393-2)

**VOL. 2: DOOM TPB...$12.99**
(ISBN: 0-7851-1457-2)

**VOL. 3: N-ZONE TPB...$12.99**
(ISBN: 0-7851-1495-5)

**VOL. 4: INHUMAN TPB...$12.99**
(ISBN: 0-7851-1667-2)

**VOL. 5: CROSSOVER TPB...$12.99**
(ISBN: 0-7851-1802-0)

**VOL. 6: FRIGHTFUL TPB...$14.99**
(ISBN: 0-7851-2017-3)

## ULTIMATE GALACTUS

**VOL. 1: NIGHTMARE TPB...$12.99**
(ISBN: 0-7851-1497-1)

**VOL. 2: SECRET TPB...$12.99**
(ISBN: 0-7851-1660-5)

**VOL. 3: EXTINCTION TPB...$12.99**
(ISBN: 0-7851-1496-3)

## ULTIMATE SPIDER-MAN

**VOL. 1: POWER & RESPONSIBILITY TPB...$14.95**
(ISBN: 0-7851-0786-X)

**VOL. 2: LEARNING CURVE TPB...$12.99**
(ISBN: 0-7851-0820-3)

**VOL. 3: DOUBLE TROUBLE TPB...$17.95**
(ISBN: 0-7851-0879-3)

**VOL. 4: LEGACY TPB...$14.99**
(ISBN: 0-7851-0968-4)

**VOL. 5: PUBLIC SCRUTINY TPB...$11.99**
(ISBN: 0-7851-1087-9)

**VOL. 6: VENOM TPB...$15.99**
(ISBN: 0-7851-1094-1)

**VOL. 7: IRRESPONSIBLE TPB...$12.99**
(ISBN: 0-7851-1092-5)

**VOL. 8: CATS & KINGS TPB...$17.99**
(ISBN: 0-7851-1250-2)

**VOL. 9: ULTIMATE SIX TPB...$17.99**
(ISBN: 0-7851-1312-6)

**VOL. 10: HOLLYWOOD TPB...$12.99**
(ISBN: 0-7851-1402-5)

**VOL. 11: CARNAGE TPB...$12.99**
(ISBN: 0-7851-1403-3)

**VOL. 12: SUPERSTARS TPB...$12.99**
(ISBN: 0-7851-1629-X)

**VOL. 13: HOBGOBLIN TPB...$12.99**
(ISBN: 0-7851-1647-8)

**VOL.14: WARRIORS TPB...$17.99**
(ISBN: 0-7851-1680-X)

**VOL.15: SILVER SABLE TPB...$15.99**
(ISBN: 0-7851-1681-8)

**VOL.16: DEADPOOL TPB...$15.99**
(ISBN: 0-7851-1927-2)

## ULTIMATE X-MEN

**VOL. 1: THE TOMORROW PEOPLE TPB...$14.95**
(ISBN: 0-7851-0788-6)

**VOL. 2: RETURN TO WEAPON X TPB...$14.95**
(ISBN: 0-7851-0868-8)

**VOL. 3: WORLD TOUR TPB...$17.99**
(ISBN: 0-7851-0961-7)

**VOL. 4: HELLFIRE & BRIMSTONE TPB...$12.99**
(ISBN: 0-7851-1089-5)

**VOL. 5: ULTIMATE WAR TPB...$10.99**
(ISBN: 0-7851-1129-8)

**VOL. 6: RETURN OF THE KING TPB...$16.99**
(ISBN: 0-7851-1091-7)

**VOL. 7: BLOCKBUSTER TPB...$12.99**
(ISBN: 0-7851-1219-7)

**VOL. 8: NEW MUTANTS TPB...$12.99**
(ISBN: 0-7851-1161-1)

**VOL. 9: THE TEMPEST TPB...$10.99**
(ISBN: 0-7851-1404-1)

**VOL. 10: CRY WOLF TPB...$8.99**
(ISBN: 0-7851-1405-X)

**VOL. 11: THE MOST DANGEROUS GAME TPB...$12.99**
(ISBN: 0-7851-1659-1)

**VOL. 12: HARD LESSONS TPB...$12.99**
(ISBN: 0-7851-1801-2)

**VOL. 13: MAGNETIC NORTH TPB...$12.99**
(ISBN: 0-7851-1906-X)

**VOL. 14: PHOENIX? TPB...$14.99**
(ISBN: 0-7851-2019-X)

For a comic store near you, call 1·888·comicbook.

# HIS NAME: THE MAGICIAN!

He's a media darling, a vital part of the X-Men dynamic and the newest member of the team. Watch the Magician live up to his name in ways you could never conceive. There is more — much, much more about this new mutant than any suspect. Meanwhile, a tormented Jean Grey is having great difficulty dealing with the results of the Shi'ar testing. Elsewhere... Dazzler stirs.

Collecting *Ultimate X-Men* #72-74 and Annual #2 — written by Robert Kirkman (*Marvel Zombies*), and illustrated by Tom Raney (*Ultimate Secret*) and Salvador Larroca (*X-Men*).

ISBN 0-7851-2020-3

**MARVEL**®

$11.99 US    $19.25 CAN

9 780785 120209    51199

T+